THE SEER COLLECTION

Articles of Divine Revelation

Volume I

Dr. Gregory Pittman Sr.

THE SEER COLLECTION

Articles of Divine Revelation Volume I

Compiled by Dr. Gregory Pittman Sr.

© Copyright 2025

Printed in the United States of America All rights reserved

No part of this book can be reproduced without the express written permission from the author, except in the case of brief quotations, critical articles or reviews.

GPS PUBLISHING L.L.C.

1315 Oakfield Dr. Ste 2914

Brandon, FL 33509

gpspublishing2662@gmail.com

All scripture unless otherwise noted are from the King James version of the Bible.

ISBN 979-8-9899-177-1-6

The Seer Collection Volume I is a select compilations of Divine Revelations given to various men and women of God from diverse stations in life. To bring forth revelation knowledge into the earth from a heavenly source. These are Holy Spirit guided words, to teach, preach and instruct, edify, rebuke, (Ephesians 4:12-15; Proverbs 27:5; 1 Timothy 4:2).

All of the contributing authors received their messages directly from God and wrote by the inspiration of the Spirit of Truth. No one asked to submit any articles for publication, but did give their consent for publication in The Seer, on the condition that their articles of revelation be published in its original entirety. Only minor grammatical editing was done in fewer than three cases.

It is our hope that you receive this collection of revelation and that it moves you toward a greater relationship with the Lord Jesus Christ. Your fellow labor in Christ.

Dr. Gregory Pittman Sr.

Table of Contents

I. Man's response to the Kingdom of God 7

II. The Pursuit of Happiness 11

IIII. Now Faith Is 19

IV. Advancing in the Kingdom 27

V. Who is God…Semper Idem 35

VI. Thinking like God 43

VII. Culture Change 48

VIII. The Institutionalized Church 58

IX. America the beautiful stained with lust 71

X. When the wicked rule 84

XI. I was born this way 116

XII. Transforming your world 128

XIII. The wrath of God is revealed against 141

XIV. In tune with Christ 151

XV. The war against truth 162

XVI. Hollowed be thy Name 167

I

Man's response to the Kingdom of God

Written by

Prophet Dr. Gregory Pittman Sr.

"Blessed are You, LORD God of Israel, our Father, forever and ever. Yours, O LORD, is the greatness, The power and the glory, The victory and the majesty; For all that is in heaven and in earth is Yours; Yours is the kingdom, O LORD, And You are exalted as head over all. Both riches and honor come from You, And You reign over all. In Your hand is power and might; In Your hand it is to make great And to give strength to all. "Now therefore, our God, we thank You And praise Your glorious name. But who am I, and who are my people, that we should be able to offer so willingly as this? For all things come from You, And of Your own we have given

You." (1Chronicles 29:10-14 NKJV, New Spirit-Filled Life Bible.)

We are accountable for the earth. God has collaborated with His redeemed to assist in the re-establishment of His "Kingdom rule" on earth. Jesus taught, preached, and ministered proclaiming, "The time is fulfilled, and the kingdom of God is at hand: repent, and believe the gospel." His earthly ministry was to be the Savior who sacrifices His life to redeem humanity that they can know the divine order and its original purpose. If we understood the dynamics of Christian life and ministry then we would understand the "Kingdom of God." Bishop Eddie Long makes a stupendous proclamation in his book "Taking Authority." He declares, "I am here to takeover, not to take sides. I have no room for compromise. This is a brand-new way of life; this is a whole new way of thinking." From the moment I read this statement I made it my own, it became not only my motto, but it is my way of thinking. If each believer stood firm on such a statement of belief, we would turn this world upside down. We would truly become more than conquerors, and the kingdom of God would be manifested throughout the entire earth.

Our response to the Kingdom of God is first and foremost, the acknowledgement that God is king, He is sovereign, and nothing will be accomplished without submission to Him.

"Yours, O LORD, is the greatness, The power and the glory, The victory and the majesty; For all that is in heaven and in the earth is Yours; Yours is the kingdom, O LORD, And You are exalted as head above all." (1 Chronicles 29:11 NKJV). God is the provider of the resources and He has ordained us to be the administrators, we are ambassadors of the kingdom of Heaven, and emissaries of that Kingdom on earth. He is the source of all things and we are His representatives, His spokesperson. *We were "…made…to have dominion over the works of (His) your hands; (and He has) put all things under His feet…"*

II

The Pursuit of Happiness

Written by

Prophet Dr. Gregory Pittman Sr.

"But seek his kingdom, and these things will be given to you as well."

The pursuit of happiness is a pursuit of the better thing's life has to offer. There is no one who rejects life necessities, we all have needs, some greater or more pressing than others. But each of us from the moment we are born we are indoctrinated, brainwashed into believing that we must pursue that which makes life easier, and more fulfilling. Many pursue riches, power, wealth, fame, entertainment, and the pleasures of the flesh as well as inordinate desires. Some pursue the achievement of things to the detriment of their fellow man. The pursuit of happiness is the pursuit of a life of accomplishment.

The late Bishop James F. Copeland once said,

"Happiness is based upon happenings." Pursuing those things, which makes you happy never, will satisfy your innermost being where selfish desires do not fulfill. The pursuit of genuine happiness is the pursuit of our original intent; it is the reason why we were created. If we desire to achieve total satisfaction, we must pursue our original mission as given by God. That mission as given by Jesus Christ during His sermon on the mount was to seek first the kingdom of

God… His command to seek is a command to be or, go about with great desire, to endeavor, enquire to require, the kingdom of God. It implies a search for something hidden; and involves the idea of urgent need. It is an earnest pursuit, which never ends. He states that this pursuit is to be foremost in importance, before any other person or thing. It is paramount, it is superior, and it is supreme, consummate, unequaled, unrivaled, before any and everything. Before anything else in order of preceding or consideration. We are to seek first, that means we are to go after. Our primary goal is to advance, to press, to drive forward, to go in search of, to look for. It is a pursuit of God, His kingdom and His righteousness. Your first and chief care is to promote the kingdom of God in this world, and to secure the kingdom glory in the next; and allegiances unto both, seeking after a universal holiness and righteousness, both of heart and life. Believers here on earth must put themselves into position to seek the kingdom of God. However, God's kingdom will not be revealed apart from God's righteousness; holiness is the only way to happiness.

The kingdom is the primary subject of the sermon on the mount—that kingdom which the God of heaven is erecting in this fallen world, within which are all the spiritually recovered and inwardly subject position of the family of Adam, under the Messiah as its Divine Head and King. Everything else must give way before its demands. It must be first in our affections, and have our whole hearts.

We must "love the Lord our God with our whole heart."

The kingdom of God is the spiritual reign or sphere attributed to God, it is, His domain, His sphere of influence, it is the territory subject to Him as king; it is undivided territory under His dominion as king. The pursuit of happiness is the continuous or repeated action of seeking the kingdom of God and as we stated earlier you cannot have His kingdom without His righteousness, they are indivisible, because the king is righteous, therefore the character of the kingdom is righteousness. To seek the kingdom and its righteousness means conformity with the claims of a higher authority and stands as an opponent to lawlessness. Righteousness is the condition commanded by God in both the Old and New Testament. It is conformity to all that He commands or appoints. Since God Himself is the standard for the believer, the Righteousness of God means the righteousness, which belongs to God, or God like Righteousness *(the righteousness of Christ).*

*R*ighteousness is living life from God's perspective, and that life is purity of heart and rectitude of life conformity of heart and life to the divine law. It includes all we call justice, honesty and virtue, with holy affections. Righteousness is that holiness which will make you a member of Christ's spiritual kingdom. As we continuously pursue the kingdom of God and its righteousness, God promises, as we seek it

"all these things shall be added unto you." What God wants us to know is, that while we are busy in pursuit of the kingdom and its righteousness, He will guarantee that not only our basic necessities are well taken care of, but just as He gave king Solomon riches which he didn't ask for, He would make us prosper. Therefore, it is unnecessary to put priority number one aside, because He will make certain we are well taken care of.

"The *pursuit of happiness"* is taking care of God's business by expanding His influence in the earth, and occupying this realm until He comes, by living according to the principles of His Kingdom, this same kingdom that Jesus spoke about on a continuous basis, in fact it consumed Him and His ministry. Remember He has stated very clearly that He will never leave you nor forsake you. Our mission therefore is to pursue God with all our heart, soul and strength. Let us all pursue and live life from God's perspective, this is eternal because He is eternal. This is **"The Pursuit of Happiness."**

III

Now Faith Is

Written by

Prophet Dr. Gregory Pittman Sr.

"Now faith is the substance of things hoped for, the evidence of things not seen."

What is now faith? According to the author of Hebrews, "Now faith" is the substance of the very things we look forward to. Faith is the ***pis-tis,*** it is the *persuasion, i.e. credence, moral conviction, the assurance, the fidelity.* Faith therefore is a firm confidence or confident expectation, it is the assurance, the firm confirmation or the title deed of things hoped for. Faith is *"pistis (Greek)" b*eing persuaded, it implies such knowledge of (trust), assent to and confidence in certain divine truths, especially those of the gospel of the kingdom. "Now faith" directs itself towards the objects of ultimate concern. *"Now Faith"* is unlimited, rich and personal, faith is concerned with what makes life worth living. We look for something that loves us; something of significance that gives value something to honor and respect that has the power to sustain our being. It is a quality of an individual not of a system, it is an orientation of the moral fiber, to oneself, to one's neighbor, to the universe, a way of seeing whatever one sees and of handling whatever one handles. It is a capacity to live at more than a mundane level, to see, to feel, to act in terms of a transcendent dimension.

Faith is a correlation of trust in loyalty to the transcendent about which concepts or propositions (beliefs) are shaped. "Now faith is" a quality of life that has taken form in a quiet confidence and its joy gives your life meaning that is profound and is determined no matter what may happen. People of this persuasion may face catastrophe and perplexity and still drive forward and face others with love.

"Now Faith" involves vision. It is a mode of knowing, of acknowledgement. We commit ourselves to that which we know or acknowledge, and live loyally with life and character shaped by that. Faith is more than commitment. Faith is a separate dimension of life, faith is a relative position of the total you, giving purpose and goal to your hopes and strivings, thoughts and actions. Faith affects the whole individual. "Now faith is" the substance of things hoped for, it is the evidence of things not seen; that is, it evidences the reality and certainty of future things, it realizes the invisible realities of another world unto our minds, and causes us to endorse them as strongly as what we perceive with our bodily eyes. Faith is a glorious reality and mightily efficacious. It works powerfully, and produces effects, which nothing else can. It is in the highest and best sense rational, and is an autonomous attribute of life, a relative potion of the totality of you, bestowing validation and purpose to your expectations, strivings, principles and actions. As intimated earlier, in the New Testament setting faith is *(pistis)* the divinely implanted principle of inward confidence, assurance, trust, and reliance on God, and all, He says.

As Jesus said, *"Have faith in God. For verily I say unto you, that whosoever shall say unto this mountain, Be removed, and be cast into the sea; and shall not doubt in his heart, but shall believe that those things which he said shall come to pass; he shall have whatsoever he said. Therefore, I say unto you, whatever things you desire, when you pray, believe that you will receive them, and you shall have them." (Mark 11:22-24).* Have faith in God. Literally, "Have the faith of God." This may mean, have strong faith, or have confidence in God; a strong belief that He is able to accomplish things that appear most difficult with infinite ease, as the fig tree was made to wither away by a word. Colossians 2:12 says that we *"having been buried with him in baptism, in which you were also raised with him through your faith in the working of God."* This faith is a living vibrant faith, it never surrenders, never fails always consistent, always seeking to place itself on the front lines and maintain its integrity with unwavering assurance that all things are possible to them that believe. "Now Faith" is faith that speaks, and faith that speaks is faith that seeks. The source and ground of our faith is the Almighty God; faith flows to Him because it flows from Him. "Now Faith" is not a ruse performed with our lips, but a spoken revelation that rises from the conviction of our hearts. Faith is not a formula for getting things from God, but faith is in our hearts and when spoken becomes active towards specific results. The only restrictions to faith are, that our faith is "in God" and in alignment with His will and His word, and that, we trust not doubting in our hearts. *And Jesus said unto them…If you have faith as a grain of mustard seed, you shall say unto this unto this mountain, remove from here to yonder place; and it shall remove; and nothing shall be impossible unto you.* That is, even a small degree of faith, that is genuine, means that you can do all things. If you have increasing, expanding, enlarged faith, growing and strengthening from small beginnings, you can perform the most difficult undertaking. There is a principle of vitality in the grain of seed, stretching forward to great results, which illustrates the nature of "Now faith." Your faith should be like that. This is probably the true meaning. Which is in stark contrast to the faith Peter exhibited in Matthew 14:31, which Jesus classified as little faith, or puny faith which means to be incredulous, lacking confidence in Christ (derived from the Greek word (oligop'-is-tos). Faith is the key that releases the resources of heaven into our lives. Therefore, it is our duty as believers to continuously exercise our faith, and impose it upon the entire world by speaking the truth of our eternal God and Savior Jesus Christ.

IV

Advancing in the Kingdom

Written by

Prophet Dr. Gregory Pittman Sr.

"For the kingdom of heaven is as a man traveling into a far country, who called his own servants, and delivered unto them his goods. And unto one he gave five talents, to another two, and to another one; to every man according to his own ability; and immediately took his journey…After a long time the lord of those servants came, and settled accounts with them."

The parable of the talents demonstrates the generosity of God when He invests each individual with specific talents. The investment of these talents is based on His estimation of our divine calling. He analyzes our lives before we live them and endows us with specific gifting needed in our daily walk for the glory of God. Once we come to an age of accountability, it becomes our responsibility to exercise those talents for the glory of God and the good of the human race. However, when we know God's will and our gifts and neglect its proper use, either by derelict of duty or unwise use we have wasted our talents, and abdicated our divine purpose. Therefore, the gift giver will evaluate us and make a decision to eradicate the talent He has invested in us and invest in someone else who is making good use of the talents he or she already has. We must understand that God's way may seem unfair or unpopular which is evidenced by the response of those around *"And he said unto them that stood by, Take from him the pound. And give it to him that has the ten pounds. And they said unto him, Lord, he has ten pounds."* God's estimation of us is far more precise and at the same time complex. His view is on a much higher plane, free from inequalities. We see from the opposite point of view, which is a conical point of view. Which is tainted by emotions, rather than viewing everything from God's perspective, which is governed by holiness and righteousness. God points out the differences between our views saying: *"For my thoughts are not your thoughts, neither are your ways, says the LORD. For as the heavens are higher than the earth, so are my ways higher than your ways, and my thoughts than your thoughts."* Therefore, when He invests in people He expects a return, no matter how minute you or I may think, He judges results, He looks at the increase you have accumulated for the Kingdom of God, and despises our excuses.

When God equips us, it may seem disproportionate from our point of view but from His perspective, all things are just, right, and therefore equal. He does not judge the way a man judges because He is perfect, therefore every gift you have is specifically and perfectly suited for your use. For God gives according to His grace. *"Having then gifts differing according to the grace that is given to us."* However, if we neglect to use it after it was designed for you; you have just corrupted the gift of God. And corrupted His good pleasure and He has no alternative but

to remove His investment. We must understand God's way of doing things, for example if we invested money into the stocks and bonds, property etc. And in due time those investments begin to double or triple we feel very good about our investments because they are paying dividends. But if those same investments were not increasing in value and began to lose money we would as a wise investor seek to withdraw our investment before we lose our initial investment. We probably would re-invest in something else where we know there is a record of accomplishment where we would reap the rewards as a shrewd investor. God works in a manner similar to ours, but when He takes and gives to another, it is righteous because He is a wiser and shrewder investor than we are. We tend to forget that God is wiser than we are, and when we don't like something, He does we say it's unfair, we need to understand His *"...thoughts are not our thoughts, neither are His ways..."*

God is just in all His dealings He does nothing out of malice but, He deals exclusively out of love, righteousness, justice and perfect holiness. He freely gives us with purpose and endows us with the responsibility to discover, cultivate, exercise and multiply that which He has graciously given. God's economy is to give the gift to those who would make the most use of them. He understood that giving "five talents" to one servant meant he was capable of using those talents to make increase and deliver them unto Him unselfishly upon His return. He also knew that providing "one talent" to another servant was an investment befitting his ability, but because that servant "...*was afraid, and went and hid his talent.*" God knew that this servant was lacking wisdom and essentially wasted the gift entrusted to him, and proved that he was unfit to manage anything in His Kingdom. This servant misunderstood the principle of sowing and reaping and neglected it, therefore his master had no choice but to take the gift.

The servant who was given the "five talents" understood the Kingdom principle of sowing and reaping, and he was deemed as a good and faithful servant. To advance in the Kingdom, the faithful servant must faithfully use his or her talents towards the advancement of the Kingdom of God. Moreover, this sets the stage for one's advancement. Jesus provided the road map when He says, "seek…first the kingdom of God, and his righteousness; and all these things shall be added unto you." Apostle Paul also writes, *"Set your affection on things above, not on things on the earth."* Our mission must be the same as Jesus' *"I must be about my Father's business."* Therefore, we should be about **Advancing the Kingdom!**

V

Who is God...Semper Idem

Written by

Prophet Dr. Gregory Pittman Sr.

*W*ho is God and what is He? We must first establish the fact that God is, because if you do not believe that He exists it will only distort your understanding of who and what He is and what He is not. Therefore, God does exist and His existence has always been and will continue to be subject to Himself, meaning He subsists outside of everything, anything, anyone and everyone, He needs no help **"to be"** because He is the same today, yesterday, and eternally. Who is God and what is He? God is "Semper Idem" which means, He is always the same. He changes not, not because He does not want to but because He cannot. God is immutable. Immutability is a divine perfection; this is one of the qualities that distinguishes Him from all other creatures. He is always the same, not subject to any change in His existence, attributes, or strength of mind.

*H*e is "I am that I AM" He is exactly what He is, nothing more and definitely nothing less. Examine Him and you will uncover things like faithfulness, not full of faith, but an inbred quality of faithfulness, signifying an unrelenting character to be absolutely the same regardless of outside circumstances, and in spite of anyone's approval or disapproval. He remains unchanged because it is His will to be so, and He cannot change His character because His character, and His attributes are unequivocally immutable. The scripture expressly states, *Forever, O'LORD, your word is settled in heaven."* He reveals through the prophet Malachi, *"I am the LORD, I change not."* His glory never wanes and His purposes are perfectly the same, for He says to us, *"I know the plans I have for you…They are plans for good and not for disaster, to give you a future and a hope."* His thoughts therefore, towards us are saturated with His faithfulness which ("changes not"), consequently, we are an intentional element of His righteous plan, since "He is Holy" and everyone of His thoughts and acts are righteous, meaning they are untainted by sin; thus, He cannot act or judge according to anything outside His holy perfections. Since He is "Semper Idem" His faithfulness is holy and His holiness is always faithful, always the same and the same always. His nature, temperament, personality, disposition, spirit, moral fiber and make-up are not controlled by caprice, but they are immutable. The plans of God never change; and all the hope which, we can have in Jesus Christ, is founded on the fact that His purpose is immutable. Whatever the purpose of God was before the universe was called into existence, they are flawlessly the same now, and will continue to be so forever. He is perfect which makes improvement or deterioration impossible.

Semper Idem (always the same) is written across the essence and attributes of God. His power, wisdom, truth is undiminished, His holiness unblemished. Since God is "semper idem" that means He is immutable, and immutability means not having the ability to change. People change, seasons change, styles change but God does not change, nor does His word; *"But the Lord's plans stand firm forever; his intentions can never be shaken" (Psalms 33:11)*. Because God the Father does not change neither does the Son of God for *"Jesus Christ is the same yesterday, today, and forever."* God also bound Himself with an oath, so that those who received the promise could be perfectly sure that He would never change His mind. Therefore, God has given both His promise and His oath. These two things are unchangeable because it is impossible for

God to lie. Therefore, we who have fled to Him for refuge can have great confidence as we hold to the hope that lies before us. This hope is a strong trustworthy anchor for our souls. If He changed His plans; if He was controlled by caprice; if He willed one thing today and another thing tomorrow, who could confide in Him or who would have any hope in the word of God? No one would know what to expect; and no one could put confidence in Him. If God should change His plans because of an impulse change of mind, and save one by faith today and condemn another by the same faith tomorrow; or if He should pardon a man today and withdraw the pardon tomorrow, what assurance could we have of salvation? How gratified, therefore, should we be that God is an inalienable counsel, and that this is long established by a solemn promise! No one could honor a God that had had not such an unchallengeable purpose; and all the optimism which man can have of God is in the fact that He is set in His ways "semper Idem."

It is well for us that, amidst all the variableness of life, there is one whose heart can never alter, and on whose brow, mutability can make no crease. All things else have changed, all things are changing. The sun itself grows dim with age; the world is waxing old; the folding up of the word out vesture has commenced; the heavens and the earth must soon pass away; they shall perish, they shall wax old as a garment; but there is One who only has immortality, whose years there is no end, and in whose person, there is no change. The stability which the anchor gives the ship when it has at last obtained a hold fast, is like that which the believers hope affords them when they are fixed upon His glorious truth. With God *"...is no* variableness*, neither shadow of turning."*

VI

Thinking Like God

Written by

Prophet Dr. Gregory Pittman Sr.

The thoughts of men, God says are not His thoughts. Neither are the ways of humanity similar to God's ways. He has measured the inconsistency between His thoughts and ways and concluded that as the heavens are an infinite distance from the earth, and east and west are always the same distance from one another. So is the disagreement between the thoughts and ways of God when weighed against humanity, the crown of His creation. God's thoughts and ways rise above corporate as well as individuals, His thoughts surpass man's understanding. To think like God, we must incorporate a principle, which He reveals to us in terms we can comprehend, He uses the analogy of rain, snow, earth, seeds, bread and the eater. He declares to open up our understanding by illustrating the reason why rain and snow falls down to the earth and we never witness its return, but we see all the effects upon our world, we know it waters and nourishes the earth and all benefit from it in some capacity. It brings forth trees, plants, vegetation, fruits, crops, it provides sustenance in some form to all of creation, and we know that without it drought, famine, disease, starvation and death could be the tragic results. God has compared it to a seed in a farmer's hand. If a farmer has seeds, he understands he has great potential in his hands and if he plants into the earth, then its awesome ability is released into the earth and produces its intended potential, and brings forth "bread to the eater." God therefore, asserts that if you can take hold of this illustration, you can understand how God thinks. God says that if the rain and snow waters the earth and causes a prosperous reaction, so will the Word of God that goes forth from My mouth there is no way that it will ever return unto Me without fruitfulness, for there is no emptiness in My Word. His Word has no other choice but to be prosperous. Whatever it was fashioned to do it must do, where it was sent will ardently bring forth prosperity. God's word is always a promise to do whatever He wants it to do, as rain fulfills its purpose, God's word will never be unproductive. The power in His word will always be fulfilled. His promise of fruitfulness is the guaranteed by product. Whether it is salvation, deliverance, healing, restoration a believer's provision or need is in it. The rain has the power to bring forth life, that is what it was intended to do. So is God's Word assured of fulfillment. His thoughts must become our thoughts; we must first choose to believe God's word is the most powerful force in the universe and act accordingly.

Thinking like God means taking God at His word even when circumstances seem to deny the truth of His promises. We may not see the immediate results of the rain, but it is working nonetheless. Our ability to embrace the will of God is dependent upon us allowing the

Holy Spirit to train us in this kind of thinking (**faith**). *"Submit yourselves therefore to God. Draw near to God, and he will draw near to you."*

VII

Culture Change

(It's time for a change)

Isaiah 55:8-9 (10-11)

Written by

Prophet Dr. Gregory Pittman Sr.

"For My thoughts are not your thoughts, nor are your ways My ways," says the LORD. "For as the heavens are higher than the earth, so are My ways higher than your ways, And My thoughts than your thoughts." (Isaiah 55:8-9)

My thoughts are not your thoughts; My ways are not your ways…

It's time for a culture change, and what that means is that it's beyond the time for a new and improved way of thinking. It is a great impossibility to bring about a radical change in any society anywhere without radically shifting people's ways, and this change has never been done without a transformation in how a culture thinks.

As the culture reasons then, that becomes the norm of that society, it matters little if the many or the few have dictated their belief to that culture, the culture will resemble what is embraced as what is right which becomes the norm, whether it is right or wrong.

Take a look outside your window and you can see that there is a true expediency for a change in the culture. As we listen to the news we hear and see the degradation the inhabitants of the world have debased themselves into. Never before in human history have, we witnessed such a complete downward spiral of human depravity in every aspect of our society. Today lies become the truth. Today lies are more desirable than the truth. Today truth takes a back row seat and dishonesty is escorted to the front row and is called up on the stage and is applauded and takes his bows.

"For the wrath of God is revealed from heaven against all ungodliness and unrighteousness of men, who suppress the truth in unrighteousness, because what may be known of God is manifest in them, for God has shown it to them. For since the creation of the world His invisible attributes are clearly seen, being understood by the things that are made, even His eternal power and Godhead, so that they are without excuse, because, although they knew God, they did not glorify Him as God, nor were thankful, but became futile in their thoughts, and their foolish hearts were darkened. Professing to be wise, they became fools, and changed the glory of the incorruptible God into an image made like corruptible man—and birds and four-footed animals and creeping things. Therefore, God also gave them up to

uncleanness, in the lusts of their hearts, to dishonor their bodies among themselves, who exchanged the truth of God for the lie, and worshiped and served the creature rather than the Creator, who is blessed forever. Amen. For this reason, God gave them up to vile passions. For even their women exchanged the. Natural use for what is against nature. Likewise, also the men, leaving the natural use of the woman, burned in their lust for one another, men with men committing what is shameful, and receiving in themselves the penalty of their error which was due. And even as they did not like to retain God in their knowledge, God gave them over to a debased mind, to do those things which are not fitting; being filled with all unrighteousness, sexual immorality, wickedness, covertness , maliciousness ; full of envy, murder, strife, deceit, evilmindedness; they are whisperers, backbiters, haters of God, violent, proud, boasters, inventors of evil things, disobedient to parents, undiscerning, untrustworthy, unloving, unforgiving , unmerciful; who, knowing the righteous judgment of God, that those who practice such things are deserving of death, not only do the same but also approve of those who practice them"
(Romans 1:18-32 NKJV, New Spirit-Filled Life Bible)

It's time for a culture change! We have stood on the sidelines and allowed many ungodly actions to take place and imprison the entire world. And here we stand as believers with the solution to the infectious disease that has crippled the world in unrighteousness. The Word of the Lord says: Its, time to bring God's way, into the earth. We need to bring the thought patterns of the Living LORD into the earthly realm. It must infect and affect every living and breathing thing, everyone must become the spitting image of the Lord Jesus Christ. We must resemble Him in deeds and in word, as He was the exact image of the Father, we must be the express image of Christ and effectively disrupt the current culture and effectively bring about a wholesome alteration to the culture.

Romans 12 makes a transitional statement it tells us to "be transformed." For us to be transformed means we must be ushered from one state of existence into another state of consciousness. When one makes a transformation what actually transpires is that a dramatic change occurs in character which changes our thoughts which causes us to change behaviorally. When this happens, it is our duty to bring about a transformation in the world that we live in. It's up to you and I to bring the world into conformity with 2 Corinthians 10:5-6 *"casting down arguments and every high thing that exalts itself against the knowledge of God, bringing every thought into captivity to the obedience of Christ, and being ready to punish all disobedience when your obedience is fulfilled"*

(NKJV, New Spirit-Filled Life Bible)

We can't remain on the sidelines voiceless anymore and continue to allow the forces of depravity to conquer our nation and control the narrative. We have a reactionary mindset, when we should always be proactive delivering souls from a fierce enemy whose intent is to destroy lives with lies. Our function should always be to change lives with the truth of God. Speak the truth in every season, reprove lies, and lifestyles that corrupt and destroy lives and disrupt the culture. It is our job as believers to control the narrative which we have failed horribly. We have allowed an agenda of perverse ideas and behavior to infiltrate, influence and inflict a spiritual death upon our culture which has already infected our children, as well as our families and institutions. The government that was supposed to be established as a Christian nation now supports the demonization of our children. No child has a right to surgically alter their gender. God doesn't make mistakes mankind does. God isn't deceived mankind is. It seems as if our government has a reprobate mind, with their support of such laws that violate the (divine) volition of God.

We are the vessels to bring heaven to earth. We are the tools God needs to bring forth the praises of God in the earth. We are the instruments to turn the world upside down. We are the containers filled with the Spirit of God that are authorized to bring the manifested presence of the Holy God into the earth with signs and wonders following us wherever we place the sole of our feet. This is the authority we have in Christ Jesus. For there is no other name under heaven given among men whereby we can be saved. Here's what God says about His glory. "***...as I live, all the earth shall be filled with the glory of the LORD—***"

(Numbers 14:21 NKJV, New Spirit-Filled Life Bible)

What God wants is His will be done on earth as it is in heaven. That means that just as in heaven everything is subject and completely submitted to the will of God, the earth must come into alignment with His will and His way. And He has commissioned you and I to facilitate, and prep the earth for His manifest presence. His will must occupy every thought. Every deed done, no behavior should conflict, contradict or **compromise**, **His will.**

VIII

The Institutionalized Church

Matthew 16:1-3,5-6,13-19; Revelations 3:14-22

Prophet Dr. Gregory Pittman Sr.

Matthew 16:1-3 KJV

… The Pharisees also with the Sadducees came, and tempting desired that he would shew them a sign from heaven. He answered and said unto them, when it is evening, ye say, it will be fair weather: for the sky is red. And in the morning, it will be foul weather today: for the sky is red and lowering. O ye hypocrites, ye can discern the face of the sky; but can ye not discern the signs of the times?

Matthew 16:5-6 KJV

And when his disciples were come to the other side, they had forgotten to take bread. Then Jesus said unto them, take heed and beware of the leaven of the Pharisees and of the Sadducees. …

Matthew 16:13-19 KJV

When Jesus came into the coasts of Caesarea Philippi, he asked his disciples, saying, whom do men say that I the Son of man am? And they said, some say that thou art John the Baptist: some, Elias; and others, Jeremiah, or one of the prophets. He saith unto them, but whom say ye that I am? And Simon Peter answered and said, Thou art the Christ, the Son of the living God. And Jesus answered and said unto him, Blessed art thou, Simon Bar-jona: for flesh and blood hath not revealed it unto thee, but my Father which is in heaven. And I say also unto thee, that thou art Peter, and upon this rock I will build my church; and the gates of hell shall not prevail against it.
And I will give unto thee the keys of the kingdom of heaven: and whatsoever thou shalt bind on earth shall be bound in heaven: and whatsoever thou shalt loose on earth shall be loosed in heaven. …

Revelation 3:14-22 KJV

And unto the angel of the church of the

Laodiceans write; These things saith the Amen, the faithful and true witness, the

beginning of the creation of God; I know thy works, that thou art neither cold nor hot: I would thou wert cold or hot. So then because thou art lukewarm, and neither cold nor hot, I will spue thee out of my mouth. Because thou sayest, I am rich, and increased with goods, and have need of nothing; and knowest not that thou art wretched, and miserable, and poor, and blind, and naked: I counsel thee to buy of me gold tried in the fire, that thou mayest be rich; and white raiment, that thou mayest be clothed, and that the shame of thy nakedness do not appear; and anoint thine eyes with eye salve, that thou mayest see. As many as I love, I rebuke and chasten: be zealous therefore, and repent. Behold, I stand at the door, and knock: if any man hear my voice, and open the door, I will come in to him, and will sup with him, and he with me. To him that overcometh will I grant to sit with me in my throne, even as I also overcame, and am set down with my Father in his throne. He that hath an ear, let him hear what the Spirit saith unto the
churches. ...

Matthew opens chapter 16 with the antagonistic Pharisees and Sadducees. They were plotting against Jesus, trying to lure Him into exercising divine revelation outside of the will of God. They required a sign from heaven they needed proof that they could verify based upon their lowly standard. And yet Jesus confronted them with their own science. He told them that, they could discern the weather patterns, but you have absolutely no discernment concerning what God is doing in your midst right now. Look around you, what do you see? What is happening in your nation, your community, in your church, can't you discern the season, can you gauge the present spiritual climate, do you recognize the presence of God or has Ichabod set in?

After rebuking the religious establishment Jesus turns his focus to His disciples and asks a question. He wanted to know what did others say, who He was, and who did they believe He was. To these questions He received two revelations, the first was a comparison to some others who were not on the level of Jesus and wasn't worthy to be mentioned in the same sentence with Jesus. Some thought He was one Israel's prophets, who themselves pointed towards the messiah. This wasn't a revelation of the Most High God, but had its genesis in the hearts of men who had no revelation but an erroneous assumption about Jesus. But Peter received an exact revelation of who Christ is. And the revelation of who He is wasn't revealed through the flesh, as, was when some tried to compare Him; who has no comparison or equal to the prophets of the past. But this was a revelation from heaven, something that the Pharisee and the Sadducee could not grasp because they were a hypocritical, wicked and adulterous generation. This blinded them from a true revelation of who Christ was, and His mission on earth. They were the religious leaders of the time and everyone followed their lead and, subsequently everyone fell into error. When leaders travel a certain road which they truly believe is the right path, but, haven't sought God for direction, or started out believing and trusting God for direction, but somewhere along the journey refused or had a lack of true discernment, and continued down the road that was clouded, but in their eyes, it looked no different than the path they began on. How could this happen? The enemy is not going to present something drastically different from the original, no, he is going to counterfeit the original with a facsimile that's going to lure you into believing that you are yet in God's perfect will. He will allow you to go to church, sing, preach, shout, and have a grand-o-time in church. He doesn't mind you having church, he just doesn't want you to become the body of Christ, because that's the true church that is built upon the rock. Jesus is the rock that the church is built upon. He is the builder of the church and He is also the foundation. So, when we become a part of the body of Christ, we have power to tread upon all the works of the enemy, and none of his power can harm us. Jesus said to Peter after he had received the revelation of who Christ was. He declared that upon this rock I will build my church and the gates of hell shall not prevail against it. That meant the power of death would not be able to prevent the advancement of the kingdom nor claim victory over those who belong to Christ.

This is God's word yet, the book of Revelation chapter 3:14-22, paints a contrasting picture. In His message to the leader of the church of Laodicea. He begins by a revelation of Himself, He does not attempt to address His ecclesia without a revelation, He makes Himself known leaving no doubt that He is present. The fault is ours if we miss it or ignore Him. To the church at Laodicea, He reveals Himself as "...the faithful and true witness..." why? Because He is the one who testifies to the truth...one who is the Revelation of the Truth, and can give information concerning it. He was aware of the workings that were going on in the Laodicean church. He knew what they were and what they were not. He knew that they didn't resemble the Church of the Living God. He knew that they were having church as usual without the Spirit of Christ being present. They weren't on fire for God and they weren't ice cold. They had become the institutionalized church. Just as the Pharisee and Sadducees had moved from a spiritual organism to a spirit-less institution, burdened by rules and regulations for everything depriving God's people of their liberty, casting a burdensome burden that was impossible to carry, causing the adherents and even the leaders to religiously miss the mark, always failing to come to a knowledge of the Lord Jesus Christ. The Laodiceans professed Christ but knew Him not. They didn't know, because He was outside trying to get into His Church. The institutionalized church believes in Christ but, He isn't priority number one. They know Him but, they don't truly know Him. They knew about Christ but, the faithful and true witness was on the outside looking in. The door to their hearts was locked shut, and He wasn't allowed in. They possessed everything that they could, except, Christ Himself. They were wealthy, and had a need for nothing. From every perspective except

Christ's, they had it all. They were supposedly the church of God on earth and because of their position and power even amongst secular society they appeared to be the true, living breathing church of God upon the earth. Therefore, they were exposed

by the "AMEN; THE FAITHFUL AND TRUE WITNESS; THE BEGINNING OF THE CREATION OF GOD!"

This was the revelation of everything the institutionalized church is not. They have become an unfaithful witness of Christ and His holy standard. The testimony of Jesus is lost in the institutionalized church as it was in Laodicea. The institutionalized church is a church that has a form of godliness but denies the power thereof. They are to, concerned with church as usual. They devise ways to raise money to increase the size of their coffers, and have extravagant expenditures. Some self-serving, some to projects where they feed the hungry and the homeless, and other projects to the less fortunate, which is admirable and should be done, yet God looks at the motive behind the action. The institutionalized church is an organization that doesn't realize that they have been seduced into believing that God has orchestrated the outcome of all they do, when, in fact God has nothing to do with them because they're operating without a license. They did not have His authority to function as the church of God in the earth which left them wretched, miserable, poor, blind, and naked.

Take a look at the attributes of the institutionalized church. They appear to be rich, but they are actually wretched. They appear to be increased with goods, but they are actually miserable. They have no need according to worldly standards, but God says you are poor (spiritually), blind and naked. The institutionalized church doesn't invest into that which is truly eternal, which is the source of genuine wealth so that the shame of their nakedness may be covered. The voice of God is continuously calling because He wants to anoint the eyes that they may see. The institutionalized church need only recognize that God is truly faithful and wants to enter in and take His rightful place as the sovereign Lord of His Church.

IX

America the Beautiful Stained with Lust

Prophet Dr. Gregory Pittman Sr.

Oh, beautiful for spacious skies...My country tis of thee, sweet land of liberty of thee I sing...

These are some of the lyrics we sang to exalt a nation that was supposedly God fearing. In times past America gave the impression that it loved and honored God, but she has always been a nation that has a form of godliness, but time after time denied the revelation thereof. She has never embraced Christ as absolute ruler, but for the sake of control mingled the principles of Christianity with a new world order. And just like oil and water does not mix neither does Christ with Belial.

If the United States of America were brought to trail to answer for her commitment to Christ and Christ alone, she would not hold up under the scrutiny of an examination for her indifference to sacred principles of the gospel of Christ, she would even be found guilty of violating the principles of her own constitution from its very inception. "*We* the people hold these truths to be self-evident **all** men are created equal." Does that statement mean that they are equal only if they are of a particular race, color, or creed?

And what about the new wave that seems to be taking the nation by storm. This insidious decision to impose upon the people's moral conscious, character and culture to accept as valid and or normal the behavior or chosen lifestyle of what has become known as the "LGBTQ+" community. With their insistence that their struggles are equivalent to that of the civil rights movement against an institutional government sponsored racism. It is erroneous to even try to equate one's chosen lifestyle to someone born black and a system that is set up against them only because they were created in God's image; not by their free will and came forth as black men and women. To do so is to trivialize the civil rights movement and dishonor those who fought, bleed and died for equality.

The real issue at hand is being overshadowed, overshadowed by a false perception that what their struggle is for, is equality. They have equality because they are born with freedom of choice here in America. But that's not enough for the LGBTQ+ community what they truly desire is to change ethics, they want to dictate what is acceptable, in this case its, their choice to choose a mate that violates the natural order prescribed by the creator God. When He said it is not good for man to be alone, His only intention was to provide for Adam someone compatible. That someone would have to fulfill the purpose of God. God desired for the man to have an intimate covenant relationship with the woman that would represent God's Devine order and not violate His principles. The LGBTQ+ violates the original and only intention of Almighty God, by assuming that there is a right as humans to pick and choose what is right and what they can and cannot accept as right. This is not the case, because the ethic of God's character which is set, is absolutely, absolute and immutable, it is not swayed, affected or infected by anything outside of Himself, as this LGBTQ+ movement is. The LGBTQ+ agenda is moved by what opposes it. It rises because of opposition and its desire is for its will to be imposed upon the entire world as acceptable. This cannot happen because behavior has to be judged by its fruit. Can the question be answered, what is the fruitfulness of homosexuality? The question has one simple answer, none!

The culture has fallen prey to the propaganda of the homosexual community and embraced fallacy. Fallacy is defined as: invalid or otherwise faulty reasoning, or "wrong moves" in the construction of an argument. A fallacious argument may be deceptive by appearing to be better than it really is. Some fallacies are committed intentionally to manipulate or persuaded by deception, while others are committed unintentionally due to carelessness or ignorance. This defines the inner workings of the LGBTQ+ community, everything is done through this prism tainted by personal lusts.

God makes it clear that these are the days prophesied that there would be no fear of God in their eyes and that they would be burned in their lust towards one another "men with men doing that which is unseemly." The problem with the whole LGBTQ+ agenda is that it goes against the natural order of creation and employs that which is not in accordance with established standards of good form or taste. But that which is shameful and the changing of the truth of God into a lie, to fulfill their vain imagination. No where in creation do we find any other species forsaking the natural purpose of its counterpart to intimately commune with the same sex of its particular species. What I am trying to convey here is that when given to vile affections even the women turned towards one another circumventing the divine plan, by dishonoring their own bodies between themselves, and also the men. What would happen to the human race if it was a totally homosexual society? The race would become extinct because the ability to fulfill the mandate to reproduce. Homosexuals don't reproduce they choose to be homosexual. And as to the dumb founded notion that the LGBTQ+ community believes that they were born that way. Well, my response to that and the idiotic assumption that some scientists have espoused. Is there any scientific evidence that other species of animals willfully have a conscious coitus with the same gender? In all of my years I have not witnessed animals habitually behaving in an intimate way that is against nature. And for human beings who are supposedly of higher intelligence to behave and believe that this is acceptable, and animals do not, makes you wonder about the intellectual level of the individual that participates and or supports such behavior.

These are the same individuals who distort a sacred symbol of God and turns it into a rallying symbol for its lustful aims. Do you know what the significance of the rainbow is? It's hard to believe that the LGBTQ+ community does, because if they did, they would've chosen a different symbol to represent their so-called, call. The rainbow was given as a sign between God and man of God's promise that He would not destroy the world by water again.

And I will establish my covenant with you; neither shall all flesh be cut off any more by the waters of a flood; neither shall there anymore be a flood to destroy the earth. And God said, this is the token of the covenant which I make between me and you and every living creature that is with you, for perpetual generations: I do set my bow in the cloud, and it shall be for a token of a covenant between me and the earth. And it shall come to pass, when I bring a cloud over the earth, that the bow shall be seen in the cloud: and I will remember my covenant, which is between me and you and every living creature of all flesh; and the waters shall no more, become a flood to destroy all flesh. And the bow shall be in the cloud; and I will look upon it, that I may remember the everlasting covenant between God and every living creature of all flesh that is upon the earth. And God said unto Noah, this is the token of the covenant, which I have established between me and all flesh that is upon the earth. (Genesis 9:11-17).

Here is another example of the truth of God being turned into a lie, to fulfill the desires of those who choose another lifestyle contrary to the norm but, which has polished itself over time as the norm making anyone or anything that opposes it abnormal or "homophobic." This is because of the darkness of their foolish hearts.

...homosexuality is a final order of rebellion against God. When people exchange the truth of God for a lie, and begin to worship the creature instead of the Creator, they are given up to evil. When values are turned upside down and moral anarchy appears, men burn with lust for other men and women burn for other women (Rom. 1:22–27). **From God's perspective the rise of homosexuality is a sign that a society is in the last stages of decay.**

What's the solution for America and its citizens? To embrace the LGBTQ+ community from the standpoint that we do love you as God's creatures but we cannot embrace your agenda nor recognize your lifestyle as natural, but encourage ALL of the LGBTQ+ community to accept the love of

Christ Jesus and turn from a lifestyle that embraces separation from God. And to embrace the Redeemer as the only way, the only truth, and the only life. Neither is there, salvation in any other, for there is no other name under heaven given among men whereby we must be saved. God doesn't want any to perish but that the LGBTQ+ community forsake their wicked way and receive Jesus Christ as savior and He will give everlasting life.

X

When the wicked rule

Apostle William D. Carter III

Cross of Calvary Deliverance Ministry

P.O. Box 9557

Richmond VA 23228

When the righteous are in authority, the people rejoice: but when the wicked beareth rule, the people mourn.
Proverbs 29:2

Edmond Burke, a famous British parliamentarian and political writer once said; "All that's necessary for the forces of evil to win in the world is for enough good men to do nothing." This certainly was demonstrated during the late 1930s. All of Europe was horrified when Nazi Germany's Adolph Hitler also known as "Der Fuehrer", marched his troops into Austria and annexed Czechoslovakia. So intimidated were the Europeans that they did absolutely nothing. In fact, Britain's then Prime Minister, Neville

Chamberlain said "Maybe" many of my

countrymen seem to feel, if we ignore those who oppose us, it will just go away." Of course, history goes on to demonstrate that the exact opposite happened. Hitler continued to grab power until most of Europe was subverted, and millions of lives were lost to his wickedly despotic tyranny. With the exception of a courageously determined response from Britain's new Prime Minister Winston Churchill, along with help from America and the Allied forces, Hitler would have overran the entire world.

This is exactly the position that America finds herself in today in reference to what has become the explosive issue of marriage and the family. Presently America is in the throes of a cultural revolution that has as its ultimate goal the capture of her psychology with the intent to reconfigure it to the spirit of Postmodernism. The forces of evil have made great strides in their attempt to subvert the God ordained institution of marriage and family. These forces have manifested themselves in a liberal agenda fueled by a postmodern religious philosophy called Secular Humanism. Secular Humanism is any system of thought or action based on the nature, interests, and ideals of man. It is a modern, rationalist movement that holds that man is capable of self-fulfillment, and ethical behavior without recourse to supernaturalism. In other words, man is capable of determining standards of morality without deistic absolutism. This pseudo philosophy asserts that all worldviews and lifestyles, including male and female homosexuality are valid. There is really no such thing as sin except in cases where somebody else's views and/or lifestyle choices are criticized. Reason and rationality are really just cultural biases, and truth especially God's truth doesn't exist.

One very important aspect of postmodern thought is relativism, which states that all values or judgments are relative, differing according to the diversity of the human status quo. In other words, there is no absolute truth. That is to say that there is no set standard of spirituality, morality, and/or reality. Relativism says that truth isn't fixed by external reality, but is decided by the group or individual for him or herself. Gen.3:5 Truth becomes manufactured, rather than discovered. Judg.17:6 As a consequent result of this mindset, the biblical definition of marriage and the traditional role of the family have been targeted for extermination. The spirit of perversion is now dictating policy in the public square, and as a direct result, America is in a spiritual, economic, and moral decline of epic proportions. All of this has led us into the quagmire of attempting to legitimatize homosexuality by redefining marriage and the family to include this perverse lifestyle. Through his

supernatural ability to skillfully access the various grotesqueries of human nature, the enemy of all that is right and good, has successfully sodomized the American culture.

From the very moment of its genesis, a conspiracy was launched against the human race. This plot has as its targeted goal the complete eradication of humanity through the elimination of marriage and the family. Contemporary evidence of this is more prevalent now than it has ever been. The advocates of the liberal homosexual's agenda attempt to legitimatize homosexuality through its recent judicial invasion of the institution of Holy Matrimony, embodies the proof of this in their over forty years push. It must be understood by all, especially the Believer in Christ, that to allow both male and female homosexuals legal access to the marriage covenant is flat out wrong. We must remember and reemphasize the reality that God has designed marriage to propagate and perpetuate humanity in the earth. In His original plan for humanity, man was commanded to "Be fruitful, and multiply, and replenish the earth, and subdue it." Gen. 1:28a. This speaks directly to what I call the Dominion Mandate, and humanity's ability to reproduce itself in the earth. When the sexual act in particular is considered in terms of the homosexual lifestyle, our ability to procreate is heinously repudiated, and

viciously distorted into a satanic vitiation of said act. First of all, it must be understood that the sexual act, including all that pertains to it, is sacred, and is exclusively confined to the marriage covenant. Therefore, God has outlawed this act when it is participated in outside of the parameters of the God ordained relationship of marriage. Gen. 2:21-24. Furthermore, God declares that "Marriage is honorable in all: and the bed undefiled: but whoremongers and adulterers God will judge." Heb.13: 4. This means that marriage is to be held in the highest esteem by both those who are married and single, but particularly by those who are married.

The Greek word for honorable is timios, and could be translated "costly". In other words, everyone who is married is to value his/her marital relationship so highly that they will avoid defiling or dishonoring the marriage "bed" by keeping themselves from any kind of sexual relationships before getting married, and from any adulterous relationships while married. Premarital sex (fornication), sodomy, prostitution, and homosexuality are all included in the Greek term pornous, and like adultery will fall under the judgment of the Thrice Holy One.

Revelation 21:8. Again, God has commanded humanity to reproduce after its own kind, and has given it the power of procreation. Both the male and female are anatomically and biologically designed to facilitate human reproduction. The genitalia of both the male and the female are complimentary to that end. The man is equipped with a pair of testicle glands, which are housed in the part of his anatomy known as his scrotum. These glands produce a creamy white milky substance called spermatozoa. The sperm in a man is also known as his "seed". A man's seed are the progeny or children that God has put in him. Thus, every generation of man has been produced by the preceding generation of men. Every man's house is within him via his sperm or seed. This is why when a man is murdered all of the people in that man are also murdered, and will never come forth. Likewise, the woman is anatomically designed to receive the male spermatozoa via the part of her, called the uterus or, as it is commonly called, the womb. The woman has what is called "eggs," which are stored in her ovaries located in the fallopian tubes. Whenever a man and a woman come together in sexual intercourse, the man climaxes, and ejaculates his sperm into her womb. If and when the sperm meets the egg, the sperm will fertilize the egg, and at least one child will be produced. The woman becomes pregnant, and goes through a gestation period, and at the end of nine months gives birth to their baby. Hence, one of the functions of the marriage covenant is to allow both the man and woman to legitimately engage in sexual intercourse for the express purposes of conveying their love for one another to each other, and to reproduce after their own kind, according to the biblical mandate.

One of the greatest paradoxes of modern times is the irrational notion of men that promote the homosexual lifestyle who say that they feel like a woman trapped inside a man's body. Nothing could be further from the truth. In fact, many women are now beginning to assert that men must begin to get in touch with the feminine aspect of themselves. This kind of thinking is very ironic, since the Bible teaches that after putting him into a deep sleep, God took one of Adam's ribs from his ribcage, and made a woman, and brought her to him. Gen.2: 21-22 In other words, all that has ever been feminine in the man, God has already taken out of him, and presented it to him in the form of a woman. Only when a man gets married, will he be able to access his feminine side

Homosexuality is a satanic perversion and egregious refutation of all that God intended as sacred to the marriage covenant. First of all, one has to ask: How do two men, or two women participate in the sexual act? The very thought itself is a study in extreme absurdity. The kind of love, which a man and a woman express to each other during the sexual act, is known as erotica. It is erotic passion expressed through the physical conduit of sexual intercourse. The anatomical and biological design of human physiology doesn't allow for same sex erotica. What happens to a man's sperm after it is ejaculated into another man's rectal cavity or for that matter, into any other orifice in his body? Remember that, the sperm is a man's seed or his offspring, his progeny, his children. The homosexual act cannot produce children. In fact, this act treats the spermatozoa as waste material, since it is ejaculated into a man's fecal material. The homosexual act is a horrendously horrific mockery of the original command to be fruitful and multiply, and the sacredness of the marriage covenant. One would have to be psychologically and emotionally imbalanced to consider homosexuality to be legitimate, especially within the framework of Holy Matrimony.

One of the definitions of the word "wicked" is "twisted". Any person who seeks to justify homosexuality is psychologically and emotionally twisted, because homosexuality is literally the very personification of wickedness. Hence, the Lord of the entire universe has declared both male and female homosexuality to be a fundamental abomination in His sight. Lev. 18: 22; 1st Cor. 6:9-10 The word "abomination" means something that is full of hatred and loathing, something disgusting and detestable. God is saying that homosexuality is disgusting, detestable, and loathsome to Him. God loathes homosexuality!!! Conversely speaking, God loves all of those who find themselves held captive to the homosexual lifestyle through the spirit of perversion, and has made available the provision for their salvation and deliverance.

Having said this, it is my endeavor to remind Believers everywhere of their individual moral responsibility to support the sanctity and perpetuity of marriage and the family. If no one else in the entire world will stand up for the marriage covenant the Body of Christ should and must. After all, God uses Holy Matrimony as an analogy to demonstrate the relationship between Christ and His Church/Bride. Hence, there is an incumbent responsibility upon every member of the corporate Body of Christ to uphold the covenant of marriage both publicly and privately. Publicly we must become both active and vocal in defense of what is most dear to our Father's heart. We must realize and understand that we do have a civic responsibility to participate in the electoral process of the country in which we live, and the form of government that we are under.

The Bible teaches that as Believers we must be submitted to all governmental authorities. Rom. 13:1-7 This includes performing our civic responsibilities as citizens of the state. As Christians we live under a democratic form of government, and we have a dual citizenship. Phil. 3:20 Our primary citizenship is in Heaven, however, we live in this present world, and as Christian citizens we must walk circumspectly. We must know and understand that both the Church and the state are institutions of God. Our spiritual obligations belong to Christ and the Church. Our other obligations belong to institutions that existed long before the Church. Matt. 22:21 Contrary to popular contemporary thinking, human government is a divine institution. The Believer must realize that he is a member of a spiritual institution called the Church, and as such is under the law of God. He is also a member of a divine institution called the state and is subject to its laws. The Church is a spiritual institution: the state is a secular institution. Both the saved and unsaved are subject to the laws of the state. God has established three institutions, which control our lives. They are the family (Gen. 2:18-25), the civil government (Gen.

9:1-7), and the Church (Acts 2). In each of these institutions there are authorities to which we must willingly submit in order that God's will may be performed both in our individual and corporate lives. However, it must be understood that submission to all authority is mandatory whether the ruler is righteous or wicked. 1st Peter 2:1718. Hence, there is an incumbent responsibility upon every member of the Church in

America to exercise his or her constitutional right to participate in the electoral process. In order to do this effectively we must become acquainted with the political issues of the day. We must research who is currently in authority, who aspires to be so, and we must proactively pray for all of those who are in authority.

Ironically Paul wrote these instructions to Believers who lived in Rome, the capital of the great Roman Empire. During that period of time, the form of government under which they lived was an absolute dictatorship. The emperor had the power of life and death over every citizen in the empire, and there was no recourse to appeal. Nero, a man so wickedly sinful and bloodthirsty that to this day his name is still synonymous with lust, murder, cruelty, and corruption was the emperor of Rome. Under his authority Rome, the capital of Italy was in a state of perpetual turmoil. It is commonly reported that Nero set the city of Rome on fire, and blamed it on the Christians. During his tenure as emperor, Nero murdered his stepfather's son, and his own mother. He murdered two of his wives and a mistress. He had his mentor poisoned, and finally after being declared an enemy of the state, he committed suicide. Truly this is a prime example of what happens when the wicked are in authority. The people will definitely mourn. Yet it was under these circumstances that the first century Church was instructed to be subject to the state. Juxtapose that form of government against the form of government under which the contemporary Christian in America lives, and you will discover that there is no comparison. Our government is a constitutional democracy that allows its citizens the right to a voice in the public square. We have a constitutional right to vote, because ours is a form of government, which is of, for, and by the people. If the electoral process should inadvertently endorse the wicked or unrighteous person(s), our form of government has checks and balances that will immediately expose and impeach said

person(s). It is an absolute shame on our part that we have allowed the enemy to practically overthrow the institution of marriage in this country. The problem comes from the fact that very few of the leadership in the Body of Christ will actually stand up to the intimidation tactics employed by homosexual activist. Ironically, it is by exercising their constitutional rights as United States citizens, through their adoption of the legal stratagems of the late civil rights movement, and their appeal to the juggernauts of liberalism such as the ACLU, that homosexual activists have been able to successfully manipulate the legislature to do their bidding.

This has happened, because the framework through which the Church sees itself is utterly flawed. It is true that we are to live simple, quiet, and peaceable lives, but this doesn't mean that we are to allow everything that we stand for to be trashed, mocked, and ridiculed without a fight. Jesus told His disciples then and now "Behold I give unto you power to tread upon serpents and scorpions and over all the power of the enemy, and nothing by any means shall hurt you." (Lk.10: 19) The word "power" used twice in this verse has two different meanings. The first word "power" in the Greek is exousia and is translated "authority." The second word "power" in the Greek is dunamis, and is translated "ability, efficiency, and might." The enemy has ability, but has no legitimate authority to exercise that ability. This means that we are the ones who have the real authority in the earth, and as Believers in the Lord Jesus Christ, we should never capitulate to any form of intimidation. 2nd Tim.1: 7 Amp.

Our most basic challenge is dealing with the controversial issues of the day; however, we must realize that our earthly assignment is to bring the influence of the Anointed One to bear upon these issues. Matt. 5: 13. Ours is the task of overthrowing the psychological and emotional strongholds that the enemy has set up in the minds of the people. Through written, vocal and peaceful dissent, we must refute all arguments, theories, sophisticated reasonings, and every proud and lofty thing that sets itself against the true knowledge of God. 2nd Cor. 10: 3-5. This is a perpetual struggle, and we must be willing to endure until the psychological and emotional makeup of humanity is completely led captive into submitted obedience to the Anointed One. We have also seriously compromised our position in the earth by blending with the culture. This has happened to us, because we have refused to renounce our earthly heritage. We have allowed the earth to distract us by capitulating to our personal carnality. Subsequently, we have developed an earth dweller mindset, and as a consequent result, we have lost both our personal and corporate distinction.

We must remember that we are under the Dominion Mandate. The Dominion Mandate is basically divided into two aspects. First, there is the Cultural aspect of the mandate. Through the New Birth experience God has called and restored man back to his rightful place over His creation as its Federal Head. According to the Genesis record Adam; the first man, was originally created to be God's vice regent over the created order. His purpose was to propagate humanity in perpetuity in the earth. He was also to subdue and dominate the earth and every living creature in it. Through this aspect of the Dominion Mandate man is to use every resource available to him in order to express the image and likeness of his Creator in the earth. This means that we are to discover truth through the sciences, to apply truth through technology, to interpret truth through the humanities, to implement truth through commerce, and to transmit truth through education. The second aspect of the mandate is called the Great Commission or the Evangelistic Mandate. Matthew 28:18-20 declares: And Jesus came and spake unto them, saying, "All power is given unto me in heaven and in earth. Go ye therefore, and teach all nations, baptizing them in the name of the Father, and of the Son, and of the Holy Ghost: Teaching them to observe all things whatsoever I have commanded you: and, lo, I am with you alway, even unto the end of the world." Amen. There is a comprehensive imperative in this statement, which when defined means that we are not only to lead individuals into conversion, but entire nations as well. This means that we are to use every available resource to make all nations Christian nations. We are to teach the nations to obey everything that Christ has commanded us. The intended effect of the execution of this command is to superimpose the image and likeness of God upon all of humanity. Hence, Christianity would become the universal culture. This is why the only way to be relevant to the culture is to live lives that are counter to the culture. Num. 14:21; Matt. 5:13; Rom. 8:5-8; Phil. 3:18-19

On the other hand, there are those of us who believe that we are to have nothing at all to do with the world. In our ignorance we interpret the expression "in the world, but not of the world" to mean that we are to refrain from all worldly activities. However, we must understand that we live in this world, and if we are to live an effective life in the world, we must actively work to influence the system of government under which we live. This means that in addition to prayer, we must use all of the rights and resources that we have as citizens of the state to exert the influence of the Anointed One over it. Noted marketing research and statistical analyst, George Barna has observed that American society is crumbling at multiple points —

economically, politically, educationally and morally. He states "Christians are not sufficiently armed for the struggle." I believe the reason for this is because; the enemy has effectively dumbed down the Believer's spiritual discernment and intellectual abilities down through his/her habitual,

however unconscious, support of philosophies and activities, which contradict the Christian faith. This renders the Believer woefully incapable of demonstrating the relevance of the Christian perspective to the issues of the day.

Privately we must model what marriage and family really mean to both our spouses and our children. The Bible is replete with instruction concerning the administration of marriage and family. I believe that the cornerstone of both the Kingdom of God in particular and society in general is the institution of marriage and family. The question that we as Christian spouses and parent(s) must rhetorically ask is; "If the foundations be destroyed, what can the righteous do?" Psalm 11:13 Verily, our response to this question will determine both the direction in which our country will go, and the fate of our way of life. One thing is certain; divorcing our spouses, abandoning our wives and children, and the wholesale murder of our progeny through the heinous evil of abortion must stop immediately, if not sooner. It is imperative that we renounce the self-life and recapture the meaning of self-sacrifice. Rom. 12:1 The state in which both the Church in particular and the nation in general find themselves is directly related to our lust for self-gratification. We must come back to our first love, resubmit our lives to Him, and return to the assignment to which we were called. This requires that we sacrifice our several theological, denominational, and ethnological differences on the altar of Christian unity. Eph. 4:1-6 It is only through these means can we escape the extraordinarily inexplicable phenomenon of "When the Wicked Rule."

XI

I was born this way

Keyoka Rock

Former student of Christian Ethics @ Kingdom Life Bible Institute Lynbrook NY

I was born this way. These five words continue to surface as an anthem posed as fact by those who live in what some may deem as an alternative lifestyle. This proclamation has been featured in a song by Lady Gaga and had become a hit due to its message of acceptance and solidarity for the LGBTQ+ community. It poses a direct opposition against the normalcy of the heterosexual lifestyle; furthermore, it cosigns the concept that same gender lovers are biologically wired that way.

The song goes on to say "...I'm beautiful in my way cause God makes no mistakes" "I'm on the right track, baby I was born this way" "Don't hide yourself in regret, just love yourself and you're set." These few sentences, extracted from a verse in this song, are a direct correlation to what same gender lovers profess. They assert that God created them to desire same sex partnership and that their desire is as natural as a heterosexual's desire for the opposite sex, therefore, it cannot be wrong or abnormal. These declarations urge them to "come out the closet" fearlessly and unapologetically. Same gender lovers also assert that anyone who opposes their love-life is projecting hatred towards them; that if they love themselves and their partner, and are not hurting anybody, then no one should have any issues with their lifestyle. Same gender lovers assert that their desire for same sex partners is an extension of a biological norm of human sexuality.

Human sexuality has been compartmentalized in different constructs, such as social, cultural, behavior and biological, to name a few. Wikipedia gives a great breakdown of this, while defining human sexuality as the way in which people experience and express themselves sexually. It also notes that the social aspects of human sexuality deal with how society influences sexuality. The cultural aspects of human sexuality deal with the history of human sexuality and cover how religious beliefs surrounding human sexuality can influence behavior, in addition to result in the suppression of one's sexuality. It is also alleged that cultural sexuality influences how one identifies themselves sexually.

Scientists and professors have weighed in their viewpoints regarding human sexuality. According to some scientists, their studies show that the biological aspect of human sexuality suggests that a person's biological make-up directly results or correlates to how they identify sexually. A documentary entitled "Born This Way: The Science Behind Being Gay (LGBQT+)" highlights some of these studies. In this documentary studies suggested that the sexual orientation of humans is contingent upon one's genetic make-up. Some of these studies include scientific claims that suggest that the limbic system, which is in the brain of every human being, is responsible for the hunger and sex drive. This leads some scientists to believe that the limbic system can be a key factor in how one sexually identifies.

Also in this documentary was the research done by Tony Bogaert, a Professor of Community Health Science and Psychology.

His studies rendered the probability that the hormonal environment inside the womb can potentially alter the genetic compounds of a male fetus, thereby altering their sexual orientation. He suggests that if a mother has several sons, then males born after the firstborn son will have an increase chance of being born gay by 3 to 6 percent. Another scientist featured in this documentary was Dean Hamer. He is the Scientist known for discovering "the gay gene" also known as the

Xq28 gene associated with homosexuality. His study showed that genes found at the tip of the X chromosome, known as the genetic marker, determines a person as gay. He also asserts that those who identify as gay will find most gay members of their family are on their mother's side of the family.

The documentary also details the study of biologist Ann Perkins, a professor of anthrozoology. She studied the male reproductive physiology and behavior in sheep. While conducting this study she discovered homosexual orientation behaviors in some of the males. Her study initially aimed to find superior breeding rams for proliferation, but these superior rams would not mate with females. She decided to do a test in which she would put one female and one male in the same pin and then bring the superior ram into this pin. The idea was to see which one the superior male would mate with. She found that these superior rams would frequently choose to mount males. Upon further research she concluded that 8% of rams are completely gay. Ann's study also showed that the brains of alpha homosexual rams closely resembled that of the female and may be the reason they mate with the same sex. She further asserts this concept with human sexual behavior of those who identify as same gender loving, since study shows that the brain of a sheep closely resembles that of humans.

The research obtained from these scientists, biologist, and professors rendered some great information, but they all admitted that their studies are inconclusive and pretty much just speculation; however, the results of these studies have influenced some same gender lovers to profess those five letter words "I was born this way." To which I argue a level of agreement.

Yes, I agree that same gender lovers are born into that lifestyle. Why do I believe this? Because the bible says in Psalm 58:3, that "the wicked are estranged from the womb: they go astray as soon as they be born, speaking lies". In the book of Psalm David confesses to God that he was born in sin and shaped in iniquity (Psalm 51:1-5).

Humanity was originally created in the image of God which embodied his righteousness, purity, sound mind, and sinless nature. Disobedience caused humanity to become estranged from God and to begin to reproduce after the sinful nature. This consists of but not limited to, unrighteousness, iniquity, and confusion. Humanity's disobedience did not just forfeit a lineage of righteousness but created an adverse effect on every living creature. Even animals were now subjected to disease, disorder, and death and remain disconnected from their pure nature which God intended for them. For the reason of humanity's fallen nature, I agree that one can be born into any sinful lifestyle, but I don't believe they have to stay in it.

In conclusion, those five words "I was born this way" has a five-letter remedy called JESUS! It's because of His sacrifice that those who were born in sin and shaped in iniquity can obtain salvation, grace, reconciliation to God, restoration from the sinful nature, and the opportunity to be born again into their God ordained righteous nature. The truth is that God created humanity to reproduce (Genesis 1:27-28). It is a known fact that homosexuality is not adaptive because no proliferation can occur between same sex partners. So, the argument same gender lovers have that infers that God created them that way is inaccurate. Human sexuality has been ordained and defined by God but tainted and redefined by man throughout the years. God intended heterosexual relationships, but humanity has altered the constructs of human sexuality by redefining it to the likes of homosexual, bestiality, polyamorous, fluid, and LGBTQ+ behaviors, to name a few. Some same gender lovers try to justify their lifestyle by arguing that Jesus never mentions homosexuality in the bible; but while the word homosexuality isn't in the bible there are scriptures that clearly indicates God's disdain for the act, and scriptures show that Jesus clearly upholds the Father's views by associating marriage as being between a man and a woman.

XII

Transforming your world

Prophet Dr. Gregory Pittman Sr.

How do we change our world around us? How do we bring transformation to a world that is violently resistant to any and all transformation towards its status quo? More importantly how do we change our

world we live in everyday? Is there a remedy for what I am struggling with today?

"And be not conformed to this world: but be ye transformed by the renewing of your mind, that ye may prove what is that good, and acceptable, and perfect, will of God."

(Romans-12:2)

An urgent call is upon our lives to "be this" and to not to "be that." What we consider pressure to be a certain way or act a certain way comes from the struggles with the flesh. The words of the prophet rings loudly in our day when he said: And the man of God was angry with him, and said, "You should have struck five or six times; then you would have struck Syria till you had destroyed it! But now you will strike Syria only three times." (2 Kings 13:19). The message is that this flesh of ours must be, can be, and should be completely under subjection, submitted totally to the Holy Spirit. Not sometimes but at all times. For the scripture tells us in Romans 8:12 (NKJV) "...we are debtors—not to the flesh, to live according to the flesh." It also tells us that, "For as many as are led by the Spirit of God, these are sons of God." (Romans 8:14 NKJV). Again, scripture cries out in Romans 8:13 "For if you live according to the flesh you will die; but if by the Spirit you put to death the deeds of the body, you will live."

The apostle Paul now begins to add practical applications to his theological discussion from the previous chapters. The first eleven chapters he distinctly deals with doctrine. In the last five chapters he deals with practical application of living the Christian life. And he begins by urgently and fervently asking us to do something. What is he imploring you and I to do? He's commanding us for our own benefit to become living sacrifices, because we are the people of God. We should offer our entire being to the Most Holy God,

Moses said: "You shall love the Lord your God with all your heart, with all your soul, and with all your strength" (Deuteronomy 6:5 NKJV). In Matthew 22:37-38 Jesus says, "You shall love the Lord your God with all your heart, with all your soul, and with all your mind.' This is the first and great commandment." So, it is out of love and obedience to our savior that we present ourselves to God. Paul calls us to a particular type of service; he's urging us to a higher dimension. A dimension that is extraordinary, that's on a higher plane than any other. This life begins at salvation and calls for a presentation of our bodies as a living sacrifice. What does the scripture say about our bodies? Therefore, do not let sin reign in your mortal body, that you should obey it in its lusts. And do not present your members as instruments of unrighteousness to sin, but present yourselves to God as being alive from the dead, and your members as instruments of righteousness to God. For sin shall not have dominion over you, for you are not under law but under grace." (Romans 6:1214 NKJV). Therefore, I urge you by all the compassion, forgiveness shown towards you who deserved the wrath of God, but because of His goodness which He displayed through the offering up of His son Jesus Christ. It is imperative that we present ourselves to Him as living sacrifices, holy, and acceptable to God. This means it's not our way but it has to be a life that is pleasing to God, and that life is a life that is patterned after Christ. His life is the only life which we immolate, that God is pleased with. Remember the word that God spoke concerning Jesus? "And suddenly a voice came from heaven, saying, "This is My beloved Son, in whom I am well pleased." (Matthew 3:17 NKJV). This is the living sacrifice the Lord God Almighty is pleased with and acceptable to God. Nothing less is acceptable. This is what Paul deems as service, this is sound, rational, and fair and makes good sense. This is a type of life that is lived from God's perspective. And this is the only type of life that true Christians live.

Paul contrasts the life we have in Christ by telling us what we shouldn't be. He says "do not be." What does he want us to avoid? He wants us to avoid "conformity." Conformity to what? Conformity to the world around us, if we're going to conform to anything we must go through the transformation of a renewed mind. Apostle John says: Do not love the world or the things in the world. If anyone loves the world, the love of the Father is not in him (1 John 2:15 NKJV). Our goal is not to accept the pattern of a world whose god is the devil. Conformity here refers to a "scheme" and "Schematic." It's alluding to conforming to an outer fashion or appearance, it's accommodating oneself to a model or pattern. Apostle Peter also admonishes us about conformity, when he said: "...as obedient children, not conforming yourselves to the former lusts, as in your ignorance..." (1 Peter 1:14 NKJV). Even the slightest conformity to the ways of the world would be fatal to the Christian life.

So therefore, what we need is a transformation. How does this take place? By the renewing of your mind. What is this transformation? Again, it is a renewing of your mind. A transformation is simply a thorough and dramatic change in form or appearance. It is a metamorphosis; a genetic alteration. In this passage the word transformation is referring to, thought and action by which one is converted from a conformity of a worldly mindset to the mind of Christ. From slave mindset to a mind which knows and accepts the righteous way of thinking and living. When we talk about this "renewing of the mind" here's what we're saying: "To "renew" is "to renovate," implying a restoration to freshness or to an original state. It intimates the potential of redemption's power to reinstate features of God's original intention for humanity and a recovery of many potentialities of the human mind and soul as designed before the Fall. The "mind" constitutes the intellect or understanding, but also includes all that is described in the word "mind-set," that is, the feelings and the will. Being "transformed" by the renewal of the mind indicates a literal "change in the form or formulas of thought or being." This describes redemption's provision of power to instill godliness in us—

a power that transforms 1) our thoughts, which lead to formulating 2) our purposes, which proceed to dictate our actions; and, thus, 3) our actions become character determining habits, shaping the life and setting the course for the future. The path to godly living is not complicated, nor is it energized by the flesh, but it does call the believer to willing submission to the Father's provision and ways." Paul writes to the Ephesians emphasizing the need for renewal when he says; "and be renewed in the spirit of your mind, and that you a put on the new man which was created according to God, in true righteousness and holiness." (Ephesians 4:23-24 NKJV). Listen to what he says to the Roman church. "Do you not know that to whom you present yourselves slaves to obey, you are that one's slaves whom you obey, whether of sin leading to death, or of obedience leading to righteousness." And then he continues to encourage the believers in verse 18 of Romans 6; "But God be thanked that though you were slaves of sin, yet you obeyed from the heart that form of doctrine to which you were delivered." The key word here is found in the seventeenth verse, the word "obey." The Greek word "hupakouo" simply means, "To hear as a subordinate, listen attentively, obey as a subject, answer and respond, submit without reservation." The idea being expressed here is, hearing, responding, and obeying. Once again in his correspondence with the church at Galatia, Paul says, "walk in the spirit and you shall not fulfill the lusts of the flesh..."

This is an admonition to check your carnality at the door and walk through the gate of the tabernacle in newness of mind and heart never looking back or going back to retrieve the nonsense of your past, it's dead, it's a dead heavy weight to be carrying in the new life, he has no usefulness, it is just wood, hay, stubble to be burned and tossed aside. The only thing that matters is how are you thinking, are you thinking like Christ or are you thinking like you? To think like Christ is to be transformed; to think like you is to think contrary to God's thoughts. Be ye TRANSFORMED by the renewing of your MIND. Do not be conformed to this world. "Pursue righteousness, faith, love, peace with those who call on the Lord out of a pure heart." Anything else is your enemy. The

Holy Spirit says do not let your focus be upon the carnal inbred inclinations of fallen humanity, but let the Holy Spirit lead us toward a life in which the tendencies of the flesh are undesirable and unproductive.

XIII

The wrath of God is revealed against...

Prophet Dr. Gregory Pittman Sr.

There has been an agenda sweeping across America, and the world. Within the last decade it has seemingly garnered insurmountable acceptance, and has trampled under its foot traditional principles of common decency, which it adamantly seeks to redefine. It has persuaded and dissuaded the masses, political systems, institutions, organizations, Hollywood, religious establishments and some leaders, to accept and even endorse foul behavior and a lifestyle that is in total contrast to proper order.

The homosexual community is determined to change the natural order of things, to benefit their salacious desire. They have proclaimed their lifestyle as normal, and they should be allowed to love anyway they choose. I agree that they have free will, but the choices we make in life has consequences, and if they choose to live their life in God's cross hairs then they will induce the wrath of a RIGHTEOUS GOD.

In their quest to redefine decency they have rejected the LOVE OF A MERCIFUL GOD. The homosexual has been seduced into attacking everything about God because they refuse to abandon their quest to impose their homosexual views upon society. They declare that those who are in opposition are essentially homophobic, but I say we who disagree with homosexuality are not homophobes. For anyone to embrace homosexuality would make them antichrist. Nowhere in scripture do I read that God hates or even fears homosexuals, therefore, neither should we hate the individual. Their practice of homosexuality makes them just as sinful as every adulterer is, or a murderer, thief, fornicator, rapists, slanderer, drug dealer or abuser, child or spouse abuser, etc. Every one of them including the homosexual if they do not repent will have a place in the lake of fire.

How is the wrath of God revealed against...the homosexual? By

"SolaScriptura"-scripture alone- God reveals His wrath from heaven against all ungodliness and unrighteousness of men, who suppress-hold down-the truth in unrighteousness... For anyone who supposes that homosexuality is normal, is to suggest that God doesn't exist, who has set and regulates the standard of morality, and this antichrist attitude of the homosexual community when they demand the recognition of equal status of their abominable behavior to be seen on the same plateau of traditional marriages. What they're doing is circumventing true morality by trying to change and distort the way people should essentially view morality. This in effect is antichrist, what this means is this, the homosexual community or a.k.a. "LGBTQ+" community has replaced Christ. The Word of God has become of no effect because they want to circumvent scripture and redefine marriage and sinful behavior and sanction evil as good and the righteous standard of God as evil homophobia because it says homosexuality is against scripture, so therefore, it has no place in our culture, therefore it must be discarded. This behavior and teaching is antichrist, therefore they and all who support them are antichrists, because their lifestyle in their view supersedes the immutable God and His infallible inerrant Word. Romans chapter one describes the downward cycle of sinful man and yet we as a society choose to ignore the word and the consequences for disobeying Christ.

According to Romans and many other passages of scripture, it is stated that if the homosexual continues to practice lewd acts that violate scripture and, therefore reject Christ, the consequences of their sins will reveal the wrath of God against the homosexual community and upon our nation and all those who are complacent, and also those that agree with the belief that there is nothing inherently wrong with sinful behavior in any form. Just as idolatry was and is an insult to the Divine veracity of God, so the fact that He equates their lifestyle with "uncleanliness. Why? Because they continue to reject God, and since they reject The Lord

God, they like satan replace the true and Living God for a lie, believing that whatever lustful desires they choose to maintain better serves them, and everyone MUST CONFORM, and forget the Creator God, and marvel with them and satan and rejoice in the created. Even a dog knows the natural order and doesn't try to copulate with the same sex dog, but men committing that which is shameful with one another ignoring the penalties of their error, and likewise the women with women, God calls it, "...that which is against nature."

Homosexuality is a microcosm of society in rebellion against God. Scripture tells the homosexual, that if a man lies with a man as a man as he lies with a woman, both of them have committed an abomination (Lev. 20:13 NKJV). And the commandment of Leviticus 18:22,25 declares: "you shall not lie with a male as with a woman. It is an abomination...for the land is defiled, therefore I will visit the punishment of its iniquity upon it, and the land vomits out its inhabitants. (NKJV)." This means that because the homosexual communities' agenda is becoming a part of the American social order, the LORD GOD ALMIGHTY is coming to visit the United States of America with His wrath. Genesis 18:21 says, The

Lord came down to see the sinful cities of Sodom and Gomorrah, "because their sin is grave (v20). God is going to visit America and she will have to answer for all of her sins, and this support of the homosexual agenda is what may, be what causes America to be overthrown in the anger of The Lord and in His wrath (Deut. 29:23). Sodom and Gomorrah were destroyed by the revealed wrath of God (revealed to Abraham) by fire and brimstone. The lake of fire in the book of Revelations burns with fire and brimstone. We need to seek God and repent as a nation, community, and as individuals of our sin and ask God to forgive us of any and all agendas that is contrary to His INERRANT, INFALLIBLE WORD, and we will not stand for any agenda including the homosexual agenda that puts us or our nation at enmity with God. God doesn't want any to perish but that the LGBTQ+ community forsake their wicked way and receive Jesus Christ as savior and He will give unto you everlasting life.

XIV

In tune with Christ

Prophet Dr. Gregory Pittman Sr.

If ye abide in me, and my words abide in you, ye shall ask what ye will, and it shall be done unto you (John 15:7).

I was speaking with a pseudo believer recently and he told me about a conversation he had with a bishop friend of his. He asked him a question. Why don't we see the miracles we saw in the past? The answers from this bishop weren't satisfying to him and he told him "You don't truly believe what you're preaching." And he said he called him weak. He said: "it's because you're weak."

Understandably the bishop was upset and felt ambushed and disrespected by his response.

But did the man I was talking to have a point? Was not the manifestation of what we preached being seen or was it just empty words with no power? And if they were powerless, why were they powerless? Had there been a miscommunication somewhere? And if so, who was to blame for this error, was it us or God?

Now here I am sitting, there in front of him and he was still searching for a satisfactory response to his questions. I knew I wasn't qualified to answer as the bishop may have so I relied on the only thing that is sure to withstand any and all scrutiny. The Word of

God. That's the only thing I knew to present.

I first quoted what Gideon the mighty man of valor said to God when he was baffled by the oppression of his people and the words of the Lord were spoken of regarding the miracles of the past. He asked God "where be all those miracles?" He wanted to know what happened to the Almighty miracle working God. Where was the deliverer of Israel? I heard about how Israel was delivered from Egyptian bondage and how God brought His people through the wilderness into a land flowing with milk and honey. The circumstances for him were so grim that he was hiding, doing a task that needed to be done in open air. So, God, since you're speaking, please answer my question.

So, this was my opening salve, as I continued the conversation I said through the unction of the Holy Ghost that the reason we don't see as many miracles, and I presented the Word of the Lord. I explained that Christ said that two things are necessary for us to exercise the will of God in the earth. Not one without the other but both interlocking each other where you do not see two but one. He said the key to getting your prayer answered is simple, but must be put into action to witness the revealed hand of God moving miraculously in our midst. Even Jesus Christ Himself employed it, the apostles exercised it and many followers put it into action.

Jesus said if you abide in me and my words abide in you, you shall ask what you will and it shall be done unto you. What we seem to miss is that we must first abide in Christ. There is no work around. Everyone who has done any great work for Christ had to first and foremost "abide in Him" nothing is possible without us abiding in Him. Our ability to serve Him and subdue the kingdom of darkness resides in Him, He is the key, He is the only answer, He is the way, the truth and the life. To abide in Him means, He is residing in us. Remember John the Baptist said He must increase and I must decrease. Abiding in Him means that He has taken up residence in our life and we are no longer first but He is. Nothing is done without His acknowledgment first. To be crucified with

Christ means that you are dead and the life that you're living now isn't you but Christ that lives in you, emphasis on lives in you. When one has crossed over to the point that your very thoughts are not your own but Christ's, and your ways aren't yours but His, then, and only then does He abide in you. It's impossible for me to do anything for Christ if I don't abide/take up my residency in Him and Him alone. Any and everything I attempt to do will be tainted by sin because it will all be done according to the flesh and God cannot and will not accept anything done in His name or any other name that's done in the flesh, He will never share His glory with anyone or anything. Therefore, the prescription for us abiding in Him eradicates any chances of the glory of God being shared with any other.

So, part one of the answer to his question is if you want to see the miraculous power of God being manifested in the earth you must without question abide in the Lord Jesus Christ and Him alone, and being in submission to His will. That means your faith must be in Him with the utmost absoluteness, there is no variableness. It is a complete trust and reliance upon Jesus Christ!

Now the second part of my answer was just as simple and had to be infused into the first part. They were never to coexist without the other. If you had one without the other which would be impossible you would be like a bird trying to fly with one wing. That would be impossible because you could never achieve one without the other. You need the two pillars of the truth of God's Grace to be resident within you.

The second pillar according to the words of

Jesus Christ are "if my words abide in you…" What the Holy Spirit wanted to convey to him as well as you and me is that without the true infallible word abiding or enduring within us not only would our prayers be hindered but we cannot work the works of God. On the day of Pentecost, the believers were in the upper room on one accord. They had the same mind, as the word homothumedon expressed. So being on one accord with Christ the miracle of the Holy Spirit was able to fill them, move through them, and speak through them; and the result was a great harvest of believers added to the church. This happened because they resided in Christ and the words of Christ took up residence in their lives completely leaving no room for anything else but the Living Christ.

Therefore, being in tune with Christ means, sacrifice of our entire being as it is surrendered unto God. And allowing the effectual workings of the Holy Spirit to lead us in the direction that God desires for us. This is the reason why Christ said, that, you can ask what you will and it shall be done unto you. Because abiding, in Christ, and His word, lines up and is directly in tune with Christ, and that which Christ desires can never seek, anything contradictory to His will.

The vine is not able to do its work in the world without its branches, this is why we need to stay connected to the vine. We must be connected to the Lord Jesus; through us He can bless men as He would. Jesus needs us to yield to Him. Service to God and man is possible only through our abiding union in Him. Abide in me, says the Lord and I in you and all things are possible.

This and only this is the perfect formula for the miraculous power of the Holy Spirit to work through born-again believers.

XV

The War Against Truth

Apostle William D. Carter III

Cross of Calvary Deliverance Ministry

P.O. Box 9557

Richmond VA 23228

Praise the Lord…everyone!!! Recently the Lord spoke a very profound and prolific word to my heart. Profound in the sense that it produced a greater level of understanding of the truths that He has revealed to me during the many years of our relationship. Prolific in the sense that this "word" provoked some brand-new ideas for me to consider. The Lord told me that everyone who has rejected the truth (Jesus Christ) is deceived, and as a consequent result have become susceptible to and embraced a counterfeit reality. This statement is extremely important, because a counterfeit reality is first of all a lie, but more importantly has the chameleonic ability to masquerade itself into any ideological, philosophical, or theological shape it desires. Hence, the apostle Paul's warning and instruction that we as Believers are to beware that we are not led away as spoil and taken captive by any man's so-called philosophy and vain deceit (just plain nonsense) is more relevant now than at any other time before. This is due to the fact that we are now living in a time of unprecedented rebellion and wholesale abandonment of the "Truth." "Truth (to whatever degree such a concept is even recognized) is assumed to be hazy, indistinct, and uncertain perhaps even ultimately unknowable." (John MacArthur). It is now believed that the Christian message of the Gospel should be kept as pliable and ambiguous as possible. This is especially attractive to young people who are in tune with the culture and the spirit of the age and can't stand to have authoritative biblical truth applied with precision to unholy minds, worldly lifestyles, and ungodly behavior. The greatest challenge to the individual Believer today is the same question that Pilate asked Jesus just prior to his authorization of the crucifixion: "What is truth?" John 18:37-38. Interestingly enough before Pilate asked Him this question, Jesus declared that everyone who was of the truth would hear His voice. The definitive answer to Pilate's questioned is given by John MacArthur in his book "The

Truth War." "Truth is the self-expression of God. It is everything that is consistent with the mind, will, character, glory, and being of God. Because all truth originated with and flows forth from God truth is both theological and ontological. Truth is the way things really are. Reality is what it is because God declared it so and made it so. Hence God is the author, source, determiner, governor, arbiter, ultimate standard, and final judge of all truth." Hence any and everyone who has rejected the Lord Jesus Christ as their personal Savior and Lord, has reject the Truth and have opted to walk in a counterfeit reality authored by the Devil. "Even him who's coming is after the working of SATAN with all power and signs and LYING (counterfeit) wonders, and with all deceivableness of unrighteousness in them that perish; because they received not the LOVE of the TRUTH that they might be saved. And for this cause God shall send them strong delusion, that they should believe a LIE (counterfeit reality): That they all might be DAMNED who believed not the Truth, but had pleasure in unrighteousness." (The parenthesis are mine).

XVI

Hollowed be thy Name

Prophet Dr. Gregory Pittman Sr.

And it came to pass, that, as he was praying in a certain place, when he ceased, one of his disciples said unto him, Lord, teach us to pray, as John also taught his disciples.

And he said unto them, when ye pray, say, Our Father which art in heaven, hallowed be thy name. Thy kingdom come. Thy will be done, as in heaven, so in earth. Give us day by day our daily bread. And forgive us our sins; for we also forgive every one that is indebted to us. And lead us not into temptation; but deliver us from evil (Luke 11:1-4).

Matthew in his gospel records it in this manner: And when thou prayest, thou shalt not be as the hypocrites are: for they love to pray standing in the synagogues and in the corners of the streets, that they may be seen of men. Verily I say unto you, they have their reward.

But thou, when thou prayest, enter into thy closet, and when thou hast shut thy door, pray to thy Father which is in secret; and thy Father which seeth in secret shall reward thee openly. But when ye pray, use not vain repetitions, as the heathen do: for they think that they shall be heard for their much speaking. Be not ye therefore like unto them: for your Father knoweth what things ye have need of, before ye ask him. After this manner therefore pray ye: Our Father which art in heaven, Hallowed be thy name. Thy kingdom come. Thy will be done in earth, as it is in heaven. Give us this day our daily bread. And forgive us our debts, as we forgive our debtors. And lead us not into temptation, but deliver us from evil: For thine is the kingdom, and the power, and the glory, forever. Amen (Matthew 6:5-13).

We have been taught that this is the Lord's prayer. It is a very good prayer. It seems to touch every aspect of our life and meets our physical as well as spiritual needs. Here's my dilemma, we apparently, received our daily bread, we have been forgiven, we have forgiven those who have trespassed against us, but all of this is emptiness. It's just words on a piece a paper that we quote and think that we have received what we have just
prayed for.

Can I just burst your bubble? I'm about to totally wreck your theology. We have condition ourselves to believe in a false conclusion that what we have prayed has come into existence in our lives. When the truth is that we haven't brought, any of what we have apparently prayed for into existence. This prayer has ushered us into a place of legalism. We have been performance based, instead of being led by the Spirit of God.

We are so me focused, that we forget that the focus of this prayer was never about you and I but it has always been God centered. It has always been God's agenda to bring His presence into the earth. Not so we could petition God to meet our every want and desire. He does desire to meet every one our needs, but not at the expense of His Glory. I believe that God would allow us to perish before He would share His glory with us. The chief agenda has always been His presence in the earth.

Isaiah records a heavenly vision where he was in the presence of God. In the heavenlies where he was taken, he heard a word which he responded to. He said here am I send, me. Where was he going to be sent and why? He was going to earth to fulfill the plan of the Most Holy God. It is the same plan that Jesus talks about in the prayer of Matthew chapter six, and Luke chapter 11. Isaiah sums it up this way: "And one cried unto another, and said, Holy, holy, holy, is the LORD of hosts: the whole earth is full of his glory." (Isaiah 6:3). (***His Glory is the fulness of the whole earth... Psalms 72:19b and let the whole earth be filled with His glory...Numbers* 14:2 *But as truly as I live, all the earth shall be filled with the glory of the LORD).*** The plan was to bring heaven to earth. Isaiah witnessed the glorious presence of the Living God and experienced changed, and recognized that the whole earth was lacking in experiencing the manifested presence of God. His experienced led him to a revelation that the lack of holiness in the earth was a hindrance to every victory in the earth. We want to blame God for the sorrows that are taking place in the world, when we have the power to rid the world of all pain and suffering. Men refuse to usher in the presence of His Holiness because they still want to embrace their own solutions to their self-inflicted troubles.

This statement is true that I am about to make, but it isn't unchangeable. "The world can never experience the kingdom of God unless, or until, God's name is Hallowed in the earth.

Unless believers can first Hallow God in their respective lives first, then in their churches, then how can the world receive what has not been revealed in us. When we fail to Hollow God's name, we fail to bring Him glory, and we fail to provide a vehicle through which He has Holy access to make Himself known in the earth. In our ignorance we have neglect to do that which is essential for that which is convenient.

Take for instance Adam and Eve. They were given dominion over the earth. God's presence was there with them. Until one day they became self-centered. They began to look at themselves as less than a child of God, and lacking something essential to usher them in a place they already were in. Instead of turning unto the presence of Elohim, they turned to self, and reasoned with self about the inadequateness they were experiencing. Knowing full well of the consequences of rebellion against God, was death. How do I know this? Because Adam and Eve were not created stupid beings. They were created in the image and likeness of God. Which means they had intellect, authority, and God consciousness. If they didn't, there would be no reason to hide themselves from Him. They hid because they became self-conscious and not God conscious. They knew that they were naked, and they were ashamed, that didn't come from God. That's why the question was asked: "who told you, you were naked? Prior to this event they were naked but there was no shame because there was no sin. The knowledge of good and evil brought about the expulsion of a sinless society and the manifested presence in the earth. What do I mean by this? At that very moment there was a rift between heaven and earth. Earth was no longer in complete conformity with heaven, but now the inhabitants of the earth was more aligned with the knowledge of good and evil then with the glorious presence of the Living God.

When God's name is "Hallowed" it means the presence of God is ushered in, His absolute attributes and character are present at that very moment and place. He has completely stepped into the moment and taken up residence and the place has now become, His domain, under His sovereign authority. When Moses went to the mountain top God said to Him, "...*Draw not nigh hither: put off thy shoes from off thy feet, for the place whereon thou standest is holy ground.*" (Exodus 3:5).

We witness the presence of God at mount Sinai and also at the dedication of the tabernacle and Solomon's temple.

Exodus 19 reveals to us the manifested presence of God coming down onto mount Sinai:

Now therefore, if ye will obey my voice indeed, and keep my covenant, then ye shall be a peculiar treasure unto me above all people: for all the earth is mine:

And ye shall be unto me a kingdom of priests, and a holy nation. These are the words which thou shalt speak unto the children of Israel.

And Moses came and called for the elders of the people, and laid before their faces all these words which the LORD commanded him. And all the people answered together, and said, All that the LORD hath spoken we will do. And Moses returned the words of the people unto the LORD. And the LORD said unto Moses, Lo, I come unto thee in a thick cloud, that the people may hear when I speak with thee, and believe thee forever. And Moses told the words of the people unto the LORD. And the LORD said unto Moses, Go unto the people, and sanctify them today and tomorrow, and let them wash their clothes, And be ready against the third day: for the third day the LORD will come down in the sight of all the people upon mount Sinai.

And Moses went down from the mount unto the people, and sanctified the people; and they washed their clothes.

And he said unto the people, Be ready against the third day: come not at your wives.

And it came to pass on the third day in the morning, that there were thunders and lightnings, and a thick cloud upon the mount, and the voice of the trumpet exceeding loud;

so that all the people that was in the camp trembled.

And Moses brought forth the people out of the camp to meet with God; and they stood at the nether part of the mount.

And mount Sinai was altogether on a smoke, because the LORD descended upon it in fire: and the smoke thereof ascended as the smoke of a furnace, and the whole mount quaked greatly.

And when the voice of the trumpet sounded long, and waxed louder and louder, Moses spake, and God answered him by a voice.

And the LORD came down upon mount Sinai, on the top of the mount: and the LORD called Moses up to the top of the mount... (Exodus 19:6-20)."

Exodus 40:34-35 tells us about the glory of God in the earth, in the tabernacle in the wilderness.

"Then a cloud covered the tent of the congregation, and the glory of the LORD filled the tabernacle. And Moses was not able to enter into the tent of the congregation,

because the cloud abode thereon, and the glory of the LORD filled the tabernacle."

And again, we witness God's Shekinah in 2 Chronicles 5:13-14,

"It came even to pass, as the trumpeters and singers were as one, to make one sound to be heard in praising and thanking the LORD; and when they lifted up their voice with the trumpets and cymbals and instruments of musick, and praised the LORD, saying, For he is good; for his mercy endureth forever: that then the house was filled with a cloud, even the house of the LORD; So that the priests could not stand to minister by reason of the cloud: for the glory of the LORD had filled the house of God."

Elijah the prophet ushered in the presence of God back into Israel when, he hallowed the name of the Lord at Mount Caramel.

And Elijah said unto all the people, Come near unto me. And all the people came near unto him. And he repaired the altar of the LORD that was broken down. And Elijah took twelve stones, according to the number of the tribes of the sons of Jacob, unto whom the word of the LORD came, saying, Israel shall be thy name: And with the stones he built an altar in the name of the LORD: and he made a trench about the altar, as great as would contain two measures of seed.

And he put the wood in order, and cut the bullock in pieces, and laid him on the wood, and said, Fill four barrels with water, and pour it on the burnt sacrifice, and on the wood. And he said, Do it the second time. And they did it the second time. And he said, Do it the third time. And they did it the third time.

And the water ran round about the altar; and he filled the trench also with water. And it came to pass at the time of the offering of the evening sacrifice, that Elijah the prophet came near, and said, LORD God of Abraham, Isaac, and of Israel, let it be known this day that thou art God in Israel, and that I am thy servant, and that I have done all these things at thy word. Hear me, O LORD, hear me, that this people may know that thou art the LORD God, and that thou hast turned their heart back again. Then the fire of the LORD fell, and consumed the burnt sacrifice, and the wood, and the stones, and the dust, and licked up the water that was in the trench. And when all the people saw it, they fell on their faces: and they said, The LORD, he is the God; the LORD, he is the God (1 Kings 18:30-39).

This was accomplished because he sanctified the name of the Lord, and the Lord God showed up in all His undeniable glory. His glory was uncontested and all that were there recognized His presence by their actions.

We must position ourselves in a posture where, we can usher in the presence of God in our sphere of influence. Isaiah saw what was happening in heaven for eternity and realized that the wonder that he saw was lacking where he resided on earth. So, he immediately cried out for a transformation because he wanted his people to experience the Shekinah presence of the Lord. When he experienced the glory of God, he realized there was an absence of God's glory in the earth.

Isaiah's experience tells us that it is our duty as believers to make God's name great in the earth and let the glorious light of Christ shine brightly illuminating everything. For the scripture tells us: ***"But ye are a chosen generation, a royal priesthood, a holy nation, a peculiar people; that ye should shew forth the praises of him who hath called you out of darkness into his marvelous light..." (***1 Peter 2:9). **AMEN!**